UNDERGROUND ANIMAL LIFE

INSIDE A
CHIPMUNK'S HOME

By Rex Ruby

Minneapolis, Minnesota

Credits: Cover and title page, © Ralf Geithe/iStock, © Antagain/iStock, © arlutz73/iStock, and © Dionisvera/Shutterstock; Design elements throughout, © Juanmonino/iStock, © pjohnson1/iStock, © fotofermer/iStock, © xxmmxx/iStock, © GlobalP/iStock, © ivanastar/iStock, © Andrey Elkin/iStock, © marcouliana/iStock, and © Dionisvera/Shutterstock; 5, © Margaret M Stewart/Shutterstock; 6–7, © Tatsuya Nishizaki/Shutterstock; 8, © Robert Winkler/Getty Images; 8–9, © Ruby Tuesday Books Ltd; 10, © NEOS1AM/Shutterstock; 11, © Bill Gozansky/Alamy; 12–13, © Takao Onozato/Aflo/Alamy; 14, © emer1940/iStock; 15, © spoonworks/iStock; 16, © legna69/iStock; 17, © S and D and K Maslowski/Minden Pictures; 18–19, © Juniors Bildarchiv GmbH/Alamy; 20–21, © Chipmunk/Alamy; and 22, © GlobalP/iStock, © Miroslav Boskov/iStock, and © Tolga TEZCAN/iStock.

Bearport Publishing Company Product Development Team

President: Jen Jenson; Director of Product Development: Spencer Brinker; Senior Editor: Allison Juda; Editor: Charly Haley; Associate Editor: Naomi Reich; Senior Designer: Colin O'Dea; Associate Designer: Elena Klinkner; Product Development Assistant: Anita Stasson

Library of Congress Cataloging-in-Publication Data

Names: Ruby, Rex, author.
Title: Inside a chipmunk's home / Rex Ruby.
Description: Minneapolis, Minnesota : Bearport Publishing Company, [2023] | Series: Underground animal life | Includes bibliographical references and index.
Identifiers: LCCN 2022007020 (print) | LCCN 2022007021 (ebook) | ISBN 9798885091374 (library binding) | ISBN 9798885091442 (paperback) | ISBN 9798885091510 (ebook)
Subjects: LCSH: Chipmunks--Behavior--Juvenile literature. | Chipmunks--Habitations--Juvenile literature. | Animal burrowing--Juvenile literature.
Classification: LCC QL737.R68 R824 2023 (print) | LCC QL737.R68 (ebook) | DDC 599.36/4156--dc23/eng/20220315
LC record available at https://lccn.loc.gov/2022007020
LC ebook record available at https://lccn.loc.gov/2022007021

Copyright © 2023 Bearport Publishing Company. All rights reserved. No part of this publication may be reproduced in whole or in part, stored in any retrieval system, or transmitted in any form or by any means, electronic, mechanical, photocopying, recording, or otherwise, without written permission from the publisher.

For more information, write to Bearport Publishing, 5357 Penn Avenue South, Minneapolis, MN 55419. Printed in the United States of America.

Contents

A Hidden Home 4
Stripes and Chirps 6
Busy Builders 8
Staying Safe 10
Hungry Chipmunks 12
Chipmunk Cheeks 14
Cozy Winters 16
A Burrow for Babies 18
Growing Up 20

Be a Chipmunk Scientist 22
Glossary 23
Index 24
Read More 24
Learn More Online 24
About the Author 24

A Hidden Home

It's a warm summer day in the woods when suddenly a chipmunk pops out of a hole in the grassy ground. The hole leads to the animal's **burrow**. Deep underground, the chipmunk has been digging its new home. It will sleep, eat, and stay safe in this secret hideaway.

The **entrance** to a chipmunk's burrow is about 2 inches (5 cm) across.

Stripes and Chirps

Chipmunks are a type of **squirrel**. They are brown with stripes on their backs. Their bellies are usually white. Some chipmunks dig burrows in the ground. Others make homes inside trees or logs. To find a chipmunk, follow the **chirps**! Chipmunks make these squeaky noises to talk with one another.

Fully grown chipmunks weigh about as much as a deck of cards.

Busy Builders

Although it may chirp to its neighbors, an adult chipmunk lives in its cozy burrow alone. To make one, the little animal uses its claws to dig an entrance hole. Then, it digs a long tunnel, rooms, and extra holes for going in and out. One room will be a bedroom. Others will store food.

A chipmunk digs its burrow about 3 feet (1 m) into the ground.

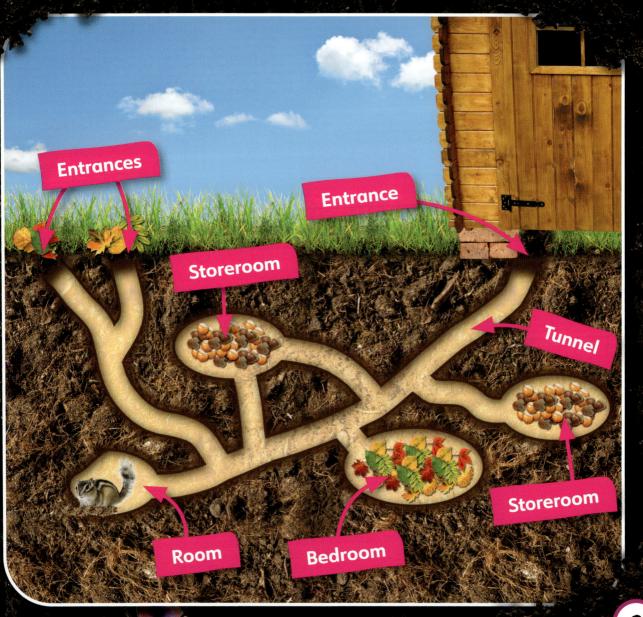

Staying Safe

Many **predators** hunt chipmunks for food. So, a secret underground home is a good place to hide. But chipmunks have to leave their burrows to find their own food. Still, if another animal chases a chipmunk above ground, it can run back down its hole. Most predators are too big to follow the chipmunk into its home!

Snakes are some of the few predators that can sneak into a chipmunk's burrow.

Hungry Chipmunks

At night, chipmunks sleep underground. During the day, they look for food in the woods or in backyards. Chipmunks eat mainly seeds, nuts, and berries. They snack on some food right away. And then they bring extra food back to their burrow **storerooms** for later.

Chipmunks sometimes eat mushrooms and birds' eggs. Small animals, such as insects, baby birds, and snails, are also on the menu.

Chipmunk Cheeks

How does a chipmunk carry its food back to the burrow? It has a pocket-like **pouch** in each cheek. Every day in the fall, the chipmunk brings hundreds of nuts and seeds to its storerooms. By winter, a chipmunk may have thousands of nuts and seeds stored underground!

A chipmunk can stuff 32 **beechnuts** into its cheek pouches at one time!

Cozy Winters

In winter, it is hard for a chipmunk to find fresh food. So, it goes underground. It will spend the cold winter sleeping in a cozy burrow bed made from leaves. When it gets hungry, the chipmunk wakes up and eats food from its storerooms.

During winter, a chipmunk may go for up to two weeks without eating.

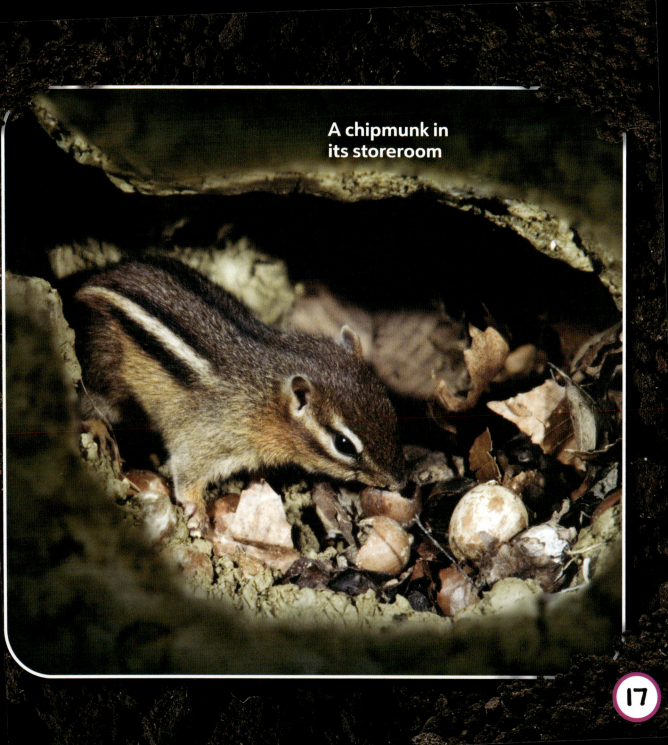
A chipmunk in its storeroom

A Burrow for Babies

The chipmunk leaves its burrow in the spring. As the weather gets warmer, the chipmunk will **mate**. About four weeks later, a female chipmunk gives birth in her burrow. She has four or five babies at one time. The babies' eyes are closed and they cannot see. The mother chipmunk feeds the babies milk from her body.

A baby chipmunk weighs about as much as two blueberries.

Growing Up

Chipmunk babies stay in their burrow until they are six weeks old. By then, their eyes are fully open and they look like small adults. The babies are ready to eat nuts, fruit, and other adult foods. Soon, young chipmunks leave to dig their own burrows!

> Some kinds of chipmunks live for only a few years. Others can get to be more than 10 years old.

Be a Chipmunk Scientist

Write a report to tell people all about a chipmunk's home. Use this book to help you. Draw pictures to include. When you finish, share your report with friends and family.

Your report can answer some of these questions:

- How does a chipmunk build its home?
- What rooms are in a chipmunk's home?
- Why does a chipmunk live underground?
- How does a chipmunk get ready for winter?

Glossary

beechnuts small brown nuts with spiky outer shells that come from beech trees

burrow a hole or tunnel dug by an animal to live in

chirps quick, high-pitched noises

entrance the way into a place

mate to come together in order to have young

pouch a pocket in an animal's body that can hold or carry things

predators animals that hunt and eat other animals

squirrel a rodent with a bushy tail that lives in burrows or trees

storerooms spaces for keeping food or supplies for later use

Index

babies 18–20
bedrooms 8–9
bodies 18
cheeks 14
fall 14
food 8, 10, 12, 14, 16, 20
mating 18
predators 10
sleeping 4, 12, 16
spring 18
storerooms 9, 12, 16
tunnels 8–9
winter 14, 16

Read More

Jenkins, Martin. *Find Out about Animal Homes (Find Out About).* Somerville, MA: Candlewick Press, 2022.

Katz Cooper, Sharon. *A Day in the Life of a Chipmunk: A 4D Book (A+ Book. A Day in the Life).* North Mankato, MN: Pebble, 2019.

London, Martha. *Chipmunks (Underground Animals).* Minneapolis: Pop! 2021.

Learn More Online

1. Go to **www.factsurfer.com** or scan the QR code below.
2. Enter "**Underground Chipmunk**" into the search box.
3. Click on the cover of this book to see a list of websites.

About the Author

Rex Ruby lives in Minnesota with his family. He doesn't live underground, but he would love to explore a chipmunk's home if he had the chance.